THE

GARDEN

By K A Austin

This book was written to be read slowly.

Let each word paint its picture,

And any morsel of Divinity be savoured.

Alternatively, read it twice!

The Garden

Copies available from:

www.christart.co.uk

www.amazon.co.uk

Published by ChristArt

Printed in UK by Micropress

Cover artwork ChristArt.co.uk

To my inspiration.

My Father and my Friend.

❧ FOREWORD ❧

Kate suggests that each word of her book should paint a picture and this is exactly what it does!
It is a book to encourage the broken, the lonely and the lost. She creatively illustrates God's love for us through all the different aspects of a garden, showing us that we each have to go through problems and difficulties, but if we follow Him, He will provide the sustenance, guidance and protection in every circumstance. It is a treasure of a book!

Fiona Castle

❧ *INTRODUCTION* ❧

I love to walk and pray. Each day I get up early
and walk a familiar two miles with Father. It is at
times like this I listen to His thoughts and when I
return home, I put them into chapters.
Sometimes a chapter takes just one walk.
Sometimes weeks of walking. But then
sometimes I can be a little hard of hearing.

✒ CONTENTS ✒

✌ DISCOVERY ཉ

It was a sunny yet breezy day. The leaves on the beeches rustled as I passed, releasing the smell of summer. A tall wooden gate guarding its secret stood before me, slightly ajar. My curiosity aroused, I stepped through the gap.

A shadow covered the world.

I had entered a garden that had been the beauty and the pride of all. But now a sadness wove its way around the scattered stones of the winding pathways. Broken pots lay crumbling, their treasures spilled onto the ground. Once elegant statues, now shattered, sprinkled the dark soil with white marble. Shapely bushes and flowering stems twisted, distorted with choking weeds. The waft of an overfull septic tank drifted by, I pulled my polo-neck up over my mouth and nose, trying not to gag.

"What happened here Father?" I whispered.

"This is my Church" He spoke and I glimpsed the broken heart of God.

"What can I do?" I gasped.

"I want you to be one of My gardeners"

∾ WORKERS ∾

And so we planted a garden, Father and I, precious and beautiful. Together we toiled and turned a blank canvas into a sanctuary of prayer and peace, with flowers that shone like gemstones and climbers that wound their way gracefully up walls. The scent of roses and honeysuckle drifted in and out of the trellis and birds sang their summer songs in the apple and cherry trees as they cast their dappled sunlight onto the daisy lawn.

That was yesterday, today a worker with a purpose had ploughed through.

The wild wooded walk was devastated. A heavy silence pressed against me as I plodded, one foot in front of the other, my eyes wide and stinging. Branches hacked off at their trunks, climbing vines drooped across the path with nothing to cling to. I stepped over the stems of snapped foxgloves that lay bleeding on the ground, clutching my cup of tea to my stomach and gaping at the destruction around me. A group of dried looking sticks protruded, brown and shredded, where the buddleia had been just about to bloom.

No!

Stately daisies lay trampled, their faces in the dirt. Red and pink Campion huddled in crumpled clumps, battered and broken.

What happened?

I stared without breathing. The toil and the joy of the garden draining through my feet.

Why? Who would do this?

A flare of heat rose in my chest. The cup hit the wall with a satisfying smash. Shards of bone china showered the grass, echoing my emotions.

Broken. It was all broken. I sat heavily, sinking in a whirlwind of despair and anger.

My garden, Father's garden, annihilated!

A few days later I was able to face Him.

"Why Father, why?"

"There are times when those with a job to do are so intent on the job, they are unaware of the effect it will have on others and unintentionally they cause damage. As it is in our garden, so it is within My Church. The work sometimes becomes more important than the people it is intended to help."

❧ RESTORATION ❧

The garden felt cool and crisp this morning and a soft mist lay on the ground. The first rays of the sun filtered through the trees and a blackbird's melody wove its notes around us. We stood, Father and I, watching the ethereal mist slowly evaporate, revealing another part of the garden. An ache grew within me, silencing the words on my tongue. I looked up at Him, my eyes full of sorrow.

"Yes" He said sadly.

"Yes. But this is not the end, it is only another beginning."

On the ground before us was a flower bed. The plants, once beautiful had been devoured. A parasite had consumed them so completely that many of their stems were no longer visible above the soil.

I looked down at my hands. I was wearing purple gardening gloves; a smile tweaked the edge of my mouth with the fun of surprise.

"Come." He said and I joined Him on His knees.

"What is dead must be cut away, so that it does not drain the remaining life of the plant."

He began to check very carefully for any green in the stems. When He was sure He made the cut. With every sharp click of each one I gave a little gasp. All went under the knife and some of the cuts were as low as the ground.

He smiled at me.

"Trust Me."

"Of course Father," One of His eyebrows lifted. "Sorry, it's just that it looks worse now than it did before."

"That is because the only life left in them is not visible; it is in the roots and that is what we must save."

"Of course."

He smiled again, a hint of humor in His eyes.

The dead wood we burned in the fire.

When it was cleared, it looked so empty, just a few short dry sticks sitting in a bed dominated by dark soil.

Father handed me a watering can.

"When they are recovered, they will be able to drink deeply again, but for now, small sips."

We sprinkled no more than a taste over the dark garden. I was struck by the barren look and the contrasting scent of living earth that surrounded me.

Looking up at Father, I began to take off my gloves. He guided me gently to the shed.

Obviously we weren't finished yet. Inside were several tools, a small table, a stool and some rush mats. He handed me the matting and collected some posts that leaned against the outside.

We stood back and watched the Carpenter. Strong arms held the post and mallet. His hair fell over his face, and out of the corner of my eye I glimpsed a red stain on one of His hands. Thud, thud, the post went deep into the ground. I brushed away the sprayed soil from my face. Thud, thud, and another post was driven into place. Beside me was a tray holding a jug and a glass. Thud, thud, the last post was done. I poured the sparkling water and handed it to Him. His eyes held me for a second before He drained the glass. A warm throb permeated my chest as I watched Him.

"Here." His voice was rich yet soft, not unlike Father's. I held one of the rush mats upright. Out came a screwdriver and together we screened the recovering garden.

The Carpenter and His Father stood together, scrutinizing the work, an unspoken warmth flowing between them.

"Good job" Father looked at me with a twinkle in His eyes.

"Why have we shaded them? Surely Father, they will need more sun than before."

The eyebrow went up again.

Note to self: stop telling Him how to do His job.

"Sorry," I whispered.

Now He was chuckling. I leaned into Him. His arm rested around my shoulder.

"They are so bruised and broken that full sun would burn them; they will need half sun for a while."

I was glad He was there; without Him to guide me, I would have finished them off.

✄ FRIENDS ✄

All around me the rhododendrons pushed out
their early buds, ready for spring next year. The
seeding trees displayed their tight green pods for
all to marvel at and the grass had a lushness to it
that had come with age.

I watched the peacock's coat of many colours
shimmer and glitter in the sun as he scratched
and pecked at the grass, leaving rich deposits to
fertilise next year's growth. I shifted. Extending
his neck, the peacock eyed me suspiciously. I held
my breath and sat rigid, the coldness from the

bench seeping through my trousers. He turned away and, dragging his royal train, rustled through the undergrowth. I breathed deeply the crisp damp air and wriggled my cold toes inside my boots.

A squirrel dashed across the grass, a flurry of brown and grey, picking at this, poking at that, gathering frantically for the winter. He stopped boldly in front of me, his beady eyes watching as he sat upright and washed behind his ears. And then he was gone, leaving the impression of a fluffy tail as he whiskered away. I chuckled at the cheeky chap.

Spike shuffled past, brandishing his prickly exterior defensively. Snuffle here and snuffle there, foraging under and behind every dark damp corner, fulfilling his duties admirably and disposing of all slimy trespassers. I shuddered at the sound of eager crunching.

Knocking attracted my attention. Perched atop a smooth grey rock was a bird with a spotted waistcoat. Holding a spiral house firmly in her beak she banged persistently on the door. She evicted the owner and discarded the empty shell with precision and a certain amount of rhythm before diving in hungrily and feasting on a delicacy not to my taste.

A flutter of charming goldfinches swept by, bobbing their way to the wild flower garden, their red caps a fleeting flash of colour, a pre-view of the turning leaves. They came to rest on a group of purple teasels and called their sparkling songs to one another between beaks full of tiny seeds. I watched them mesmerized as they danced away, their tiny wings fluttering with gold.

"This is a good place Father, where all is balanced and there are helpers of all shapes and sizes."

His smile shone warmly on my face.

"Yes, My garden has many friends, as does my Church. Some completely unaware of the service they provide."

⚜ *WEEDS* ⚜

We walked arm in arm through the colours of
summer. A light rain in the night had stirred the
soil giving the walk a rich fragrance. I breathed
deeply. This was my favourite time, walking with
Him in the early hours. I felt His smile lift my head
and I looked into His eyes, so tender, so filled
with unfathomable love. Heat flushed my face
and I gazed, falling into Him. He turned with
intent, I turned with Him. The bed before us was
filled with strawberries; some lay on the soil, rich
red and heavily ripe, others wore perfectly
formed pink and white flowers. Some however

were obscured by large weeds that were choking them and blocking the light.

We knelt together and I watched Him probe and prod, His fingers pressing into the soil as He slowly and painstakingly separated the weed stems.

"Oh!" I squeaked involuntarily at the sharp tool He produced.

Carefully He began to pierce the earth around the weed stem, pushing it deep into the ground and prising the roots from the soil. Grasping the base firmly I felt the wrench as He pulled gently and the root was dislodged, such a long jagged point. Groaning I leaned forward, feeling the roots of betrayal and fear come free of their far reaching crevices. He lifted slowly, loosening each tendril whilst keeping them intact, until the whole came cleanly and completely out. He extended His hand once more and from it poured a vial of healing balm. Its warmth flowed like liquid sunlight, beginning at my innermost being and slowly spreading its tingling glow to every opened cavity until the tips of my fingers were buzzing.

"Wow!" I said smiling. He was smiling too, but something else lay behind His eyes. I looked at Him, unspoken questions on my lips. He answered.

"Many of My children are choking with weeds, some their own making and some planted by others, it matters not. They must be extracted sensitively and with great care so that the fruit is not damaged."

⁓ *STAGNANT* ⤾

I walked alone around the pond, the only sound the squelching of sticky mud under my feet. The stinking water gave off a murky green hue. Slime coated rocks gathered in clusters and wafts of rotting vegetation washed over me, catching in my throat.

Why has He abandoned this part of the garden?

I followed the pathway around a group of trees and there on a bench I found Him.

"Father, what has happened to the pond?"

He frowned.

"It has become stagnant, dead plants and things unclean have blocked the flow of fresh water from the underground stream. The water it holds is contaminated and the pond is dying."

"Oh!"

The air around us hung deathly still, its clammy fingers threading their way through my hair.

"Can't we do something?" I ventured.

"Of course!"

He stood suddenly and grasped my hand. The distant whisper of an eager wind swept hope through my heart. We moved quickly to the uppermost part of the water where a small and clear stream waited behind an almost submerged closed gate. The meander of the stream led to the gate and then veered away, to feed other parts of the garden.

We began to clear the build-up of leaves and stones pressing against the gate, preventing it from being opened.

Now I could do with a pair of gloves.

I resisted looking at Him, that eyebrow would be arched at me again. Some of the stones were small boulders and I could not lift them, but He is strong and once I was out of His way, He removed them easily. Eventually we stood back and surveyed our handiwork. He gave a satisfied sigh as He lifted the latch and allowed the water to push open the gate. The stream bubbled excitedly through, its fresh water flowing into the stagnant pond.

"Run!" He called, leaving me standing.

I lolloped after Him, panting. Goodness, He can run. I caught up at the other end of the pond. By the time I got there He looked like some kind of mud monster, covered in thick green/black slime.

"Urrgg! It stinks!"

"Yes doesn't it," He grinned, mud between His teeth.

Most times I don't completely understand Him. He was knee deep in foul smelling slime, snatching great handfuls of it gleefully and throwing it high into the air behind Him.

"Oh well, here goes," I muttered.

Pulling my jumper over my mouth and nose I dived in next to Him.

Yuk! I could really do with those gloves now!

He laughed out loud, surrounded by flying muck. Buried deeply in the mound was another gate, identical to the first. We stood together mud-slinging, but the more we cleared the more there was to fill its place.

"This isn't working," I called above His laughter.

Why is He laughing? This is disgusting!

"Keep going!" He shouted, urging me on.

We worked together until our fingers were sore and we smelled like putrid pond.

Why oh why can't I have the gloves?

"Sometimes you have to get your hands dirty!" He yelled, spitting mud at me.

Delightful!

At last the gate appeared and we were flinging the final fistfuls of stagnancy. He gave a great shout and pushed hard, an impatient wave of pent up water forced it wide open,

simultaneously washing and soaking me.
Spluttering I staggered towards the bank, His
laughter ringing in my ears.

I lay drying in the sun, gazing up at the sky,
drifting with the cotton clouds skimming the blue.
His voice roused me.

"Look!"

A kingfisher flashed vibrantly across my vision.
The coolness of the now crystal clear water lifted,
filling the air with the fresh smell of a new day
after rain. Lilies floated elegantly at intervals
across the diamond pathway of reflecting light. I
gazed mesmerised into the pond at the many
coloured pebbles covering its bottom and the
pearlescent fish weaving in and out of the
bulrushes.

"Beautiful, beautiful!" I exclaimed ecstatically.

"Yes." he responded, pure joy in his creases.

Walking back I asked simply, "Explain?"

**"Things can become stagnant if they are seen as
the goal and not part of the journey. The flow of
Love becomes blocked and all slowly dies. The**

blockage must be revealed and if it cannot be restored, it must be removed. Then My life can flow freely and wash away all that has become stagnant."

❧ *PARASITES* ❧

I trod softly upon the dew-spangled grass. The cool morning swept through the garden giving everything a fresh and lively fragrance. I met Him hovering over some rose bushes, His hands working feverishly on their stems.

"Good and beautiful morning" I said in a sing song voice.

"It is." He replied somewhat less than sing-song.

"What are you doing?" I moved nearer.

"Dealing with a few awkward individuals!" He gave me a look that made me question whether or not I was one of them.

"Can I help?" I offered hopefully.

"Sometimes," He responded cryptically.

I sighed before I could stop myself. He glanced my way, and then stood and faced me. My skin prickled and I felt as though I was shrivelling before His all-seeing gaze.

"Do you know that you love me?" He asked searchingly.

"Yes Lord," I whispered, getting more nervous by the second.

"Then why are you afraid?" His eyes softened.

I thought back to the times I felt inadequate; there were so many, my heart ached with the burden of them. Underneath them all lay the fear that I didn't think my love for Him was strong enough to defeat my self-love.

How well He knows me.

"Why do you love Me?"

I screwed up my brow.

*Why do I love Him? Because He loves me and I
cannot help but love Him back.*

I could feel the glow of His smile warming my
face. I leaned towards a blood red rose and took
a deep breath of deliciousness.

"Now, let's do some work shall we?"

We focused on the roses and I noticed leaves
covered in black spots. He snipped them off at
the stem. Some of their buds had turned black
and hung by a thread to their parent plant. He
pulled them off and I saw the culprits. Small and
well camouflaged, a huddle of aphids clung to the
stalks. He bent over and inflated His chest before
blowing a great gust of air at them. They sailed
away with the wind and I never saw them again.

"How satisfying!" I exclaimed delighted.

We moved further in, kneeling together at the
edge of another bed where the foliage had been
stripped bare. I watched carefully as He lifted leaf
stems and stones until He found the slimy
suspects and disposed of them in a large pot of
sunlight drenched salt.

"Some parasites cling, sucking the life from My children. Others slither in amongst you unnoticed and devour with unquenchable hunger. Not everyone is who they say they are. What is done in the darkness must be exposed to the light and so the Truth will set you free."

❧ SUPPORT ❧

There had been a storm in the night. I wondered
how I had slept through it. I wandered around the
pathways, stepping over plants that had blown
down in the wind. I was following the sound of
Him singing. A few brave honey bees joined the
song and hummed in and out of flattened petals.

"Here you are," He stroked my hair.

A warm glow permeated the atmosphere around
Him. *"Come, we have work to do."*

I followed Him to the shed; we took a
wheelbarrow filled with old sticks and metal rods.

"Will I need gloves?" I asked hopefully.

He chuckled.

I'm delighted I am such a source of amusement to Him!

We stopped at a peony laying across the path, I felt my forehead crinkle, it was such a shame, such beautiful deep red blooms, washed out by the heavy rain.

"Rods!" He announced, holding out a hand like we were in an operating theatre and He was the surgeon.

I looked at the wheelbarrow, selected one of the metal bars, handed it to Him and announced,

"Rod!"

He grinned and held His hand out for more. I crouched with Him and listened to the warm squelches as He forced the rods strategically into the soil. He then wound twine between and around them.

Incredible!

I sat back and observed the small triangle of metal support, hardly visible, that now held up the whole bush perfectly.

Off we went again, trundling along with our wheelbarrow. We stopped at a bed of dahlias all squabbling in the dirt. He caned each of them individually with a short stick taken from a pruned bush and bound them firmly to their supports.

Next He led me to a blackberry. It was bent double, unwilling to abandon its water logged fruit splattered over the soil beneath it.

"Stick."

He can be very demanding sometimes!

I passed Him the only thing left in the barrow, a spindly bamboo cane. He wound the stick around the stem and pushed it firmly into the ground. I held my breath.

Surely that's not going to hold it.

He let go. The bramble sagged a little but remained upright.

Oh no!

I took a handkerchief from my pocket and wrapped it around His bleeding fingers.

That was a ferocious plant!

As I looked around I noticed other supports, some of them almost invisible while others were very visible and had an elegance and beauty of their own. I could feel Him grinning at me as my understanding grew.

"Some of My children need more support than others, and that is why fellowship is so important - real fellowship whereby each supports another without thought of self or glory."

I often marvel at how clever He is.

∽ SOIL ∾

It was a quiet afternoon. We were sitting in the shade of a heavily laden plum whose fruit was turning a rich deep purple.

I sighed contentedly and gazed at Father. I was warm, comfortable and the garden was beautiful. Blooms of deep pink and purple waggled their heads at me and pollen sparkled in the rays of light, filling the air with sweetness and lulling me into a heady daze. Insects buzzed a faint chorus and puffy clouds curdled their way across a bright azure sky.

"You o' soil," His voice was serious.

I snapped too.

"What do you mean? Are you calling me soil?"

I want to be a rose. I thought dejectedly.

He remained silent.

"Hrmph," I'll do my own research then!

I discovered several enlightening facts.

Soil has many functions: It is the substance in which plants grow, it feeds them and holds them. It stores water, supplying and purifying. It even modifies the atmosphere, adapting it appropriately for its plants. It is a habitat for organisms that break down dead plants and revitalise new life.

"Hrmph, ok."

I can live with that.

The echo of His laughter sounded in my ears.

✥ GROUPS ✥

Today we ambled, without obvious purpose. We did not speak. He pointed and I looked. The sun blazed along its path, warming me through my clothes. I followed the line of His hand to a large and vibrant bed, its jewelled flowers stood upright and when the breeze blew through them, their faces tilted, like kings and queens displaying their royal colours boldly to the rest of the garden.

What elegance and beauty.

We walked on. He indicated to a smaller bed. Miniature hedges in perfect symmetry squatted alongside each other, covered with sprays of tiny flowers of gold.

So perfect, so pretty.

And on He led me, through archways of clematis that clung to their supports, winding upwards in graceful shapely beauty.

What colour, what form.

We passed by several circular beds, pathways of pebbles framing them, linking them together in a tapestry of coloured stone. In each were uninteresting, almost scruffy bushes. He stooped and brushed His hands over one. I was lost in a haze of exotic perfume that swirled about us like morning mist. Breathing deeply, I felt the aches of toil lift from my shoulders.

Delicious.

Still further, we passed beneath a canopy of tall trees, rising like the pillars of a natural cathedral, their umbrella like arches lit up fresh green with radiant sunlight. I caressed the silvery smooth trunks as we passed by, my fingers tingling with the life that flowed from these lords of the garden.

Such majesty.

I felt His hand on my arm and I gazed in the direction He guided me. The earth beneath the trees seemed dark and bare. He kneeled and I watched His face get so close to the ground the soil dusted the air as He breathed. I joined Him and when my eyes focussed I saw what He saw. Tiny flowers like sapphires shone up at us. Each petal ending in a perfect point and, at the centre of every deep blue, sparkled a pinprick of dew, like a tiny diamond.

So small and yet their beauty is equal to any in the garden.

"There are many groups in My garden, just as there are many groups within My Church; some more prominent, others quiet and unseen. Each has a beauty all their own. Not one is unwanted, there is a place for all."

✌ *VULTURES* ☙

Soft grass fluttered around my face as I lay on my
back in the meadow, looking up at the sky with its
blustery puffs of cloud. A handful of fluffy seeds
whisked by. Sighing contentedly I pulled myself
up onto an elbow and gazed over at Him. He put
one finger to His lips, shushing me and continued
studying the sky. I followed His eyes and there far
above circled several large birds. Slowly, slowly
they descended, their circles growing smaller,
until at last they landed on a solitary tree. I
frowned. I had not noticed that particular tree
before, it looked so out of place in the lush green.

It bore neither leaf nor fruit. Its skeletal branches twisted unnaturally down and inward, making it look hunched and deformed. The birds flapped their sparsely feathered wings; ugly creatures with eyes that bulged in contorted faces.

Why do vultures always look half starved?

I raised my eyebrows in question.

"It was beautiful once, that tree,"

I waited, knowing there was more.

"Its fruit was sweet and its presence celebrated,"

A single tear wove a pathway down His cheek.

"It believed in its own beauty and was cut off from the source of its life."

The trickle of tears appeared on my face.

"It died!"

My lungs pressed against my chest.

"The vultures were waiting."

His hand covered mine, I breathed.

"Many of my people have cut themselves off from the Source without realising. They no

longer fellowship with Me. Others have descended upon them to devour because where there is a dead body, the vultures gather!"

✆ *RESTING* ✆

There was a stillness in the air. No breeze stirred
and nothing moved. I tiptoed between stately
oaks standing guard like aged sentinels. A serene
calm permeated the atmosphere, quelling my
curiosity. I breathed slowly and carefully, the
deep and earthy smell filling my lungs. Patterned
leaves floated around me, creating a carpet of
soft gold. I smiled, entranced by their bouncy
landings. Soft green moss beneath the leafy
blanket caught my eye and an overwhelming
desire to rest lay heavily on my breast, almost
suffocating me. I dragged my feet through the

leaves like lumps of rock and my eyelids drooped lower and lower, each time of closing heavier than the last.

 "What is this place Father?"

I murmured, sinking down into the cushioned overlay and breathing a last waking breath. Whilst I slept His voice surrounded me, hemming me in and lulling me deeper.

"This is My place of rest. These trees I give you, to shelter and cover those who toil, those who are healing and those who have fulfilled My purpose."

A song-bird was singing a solitary melody. A morning song. Extending my arms I stretched out of a satisfying yawn and sat up. Feeling refreshed I set out to look for Him. The garden was still at rest. I walked quietly through the trees and came upon a lake with calm and far reaching waters. Dim hues of early morning reflected in the glassy, still surface. The freshness of cool water rose all about me, clearing my senses. Looking up, my eyes brightened as the new dawn spilled over the horizon onto the waiting garden. Golden light washed the day and silence reigned beside the quiet waters. I heard the sound of a still small voice.

"All my children must rest. Walk beside the still waters, let your heart be quieted so that you may be restored."

✂ *DISAPPOINTMENT* ✂

It was a strange feeling. I had followed a narrow pathway into a circular patch of grass with a watering can sitting in its centre. I picked it up and evenly sprinkled the dark soil of the bed before me. Expectancy crackled like electricity in the air and I waited for its promised event. Nothing happened. Tutting I replaced the can and paced around the woodchip that hemmed the grass. And then, the whole world held its breath as a solitary shoot burst from the dampened soil with a fresh green whoosh that made me want to dance. I laughed out loud with the joy of looking straight at something when it happens. There it grew, alone. I smiled and waited again. I waited for a long time. Nothing. Frustrated I rubbed my arms as though they were cold although they were not.

What am I doing here? What am I waiting for?

"This place is available to all who have the courage to enter."

I had no idea what He meant so I fired questions.

"Who do you mean by 'all'? And what are they entering? And why do they need courage?"

He, of course, was silent, waiting for me to be quiet and contemplate. I didn't feel like contemplating, I had been waiting here for ages and for what? One solitary sprout! I expected more and I was disappointed and discouraged. How many times had I been available when only one or two had turned up? How many times had I put my all into something only to be let down? This had an all too familiar ring to it, there were parallels here that made me squirm.

"Father, please, sift this mess in my brain."

"Some of My children need gentle guidance to find Me, in a safe place where they are not observed. Those who facilitate a place to meet with Me should remember it is I who plant, I who water and I who give the growth so be glad for all who come your way, however small and however few."

❦ *POISON* ❧

I stared at the wilting fuchsia. Its stunted leaves clinging to the stooping stem.

What is wrong with that piece of garden?

Everything I put there, and I had tried several different plants, had gradually died.

"Father, what am I doing wrong? Nothing will grow here, I have tried, I really have!"

"There is poison in the soil,"

His voice broke through my ramblings.

"Poison?" I repeated stupidly. "What kind of poison?"

He was silent for a moment, waiting for me to still myself.

"Poison that came in at the beginning of the garden, it seeped into the soil unnoticed and has been twisting and choking the plants ever since."

"What can I do?"

I was feeling exceptionally stupid today. I knew He was getting at something and I wasn't getting whatever it was.

"A little leaven….,"

It was just a whisper but it was enough.

"Ahh."

My brain shook itself into life.

"What do I do?"

Almost the same question but with infinitely less stupidity behind it.

"It must first be revealed, look into the history."

I discovered a dumping ground for the old oil tank.

"When you have discovered the source, it must be removed."

"How?"

"Expose and wash the soil, discard what does not clean, feed what is left and it will be ready for new growth, and don't forget your gloves."

I chuckled at my purple hand protectors and got to work.

✒ *KNOTS* ✒

Over the boundary wall I could see several small bushes, twisting and turning, growing in on themselves as though they had been tied up in knots. Stepping through the gate I bent to inspect them more closely. They were intricate in their windings, tangled stems clung to each other, growing through each other. A sickly sweet smell exuded from some of them and others wore fungus on their leaves. There were no flowers and no fruit, nor one straight and upright stem among them. One of them even grew back into the ground as though hiding from the sun.

"Father? What are these?"

"They are those that have looked within and created their own God."

"Can we rescue them, maybe untangle them a little and turn them to the light?"

"The light shines on them as it does on all; it is in their nature to grow towards it. They fight their own nature to find what they believe they want. When they come to the end of their tangled weaving, some of them will turn naturally to the Son."

✥ FRUIT ✥

The colours of autumn swam about, my eyes hungrily gobbled them up. Oh so beautiful: the yellows, the reds and the light, there is something different about autumn light; it is richer, more golden. I found my arm linked with His and we were strolling up a gravel path, its small stones crunching satisfyingly beneath our feet. On both sides of the path were fruit trees. We stopped at a pear, so heavily laden its branches sagged and much of the fruit lay on the ground. I leaned toward a branch and lifted it slightly. The smell of mould seeped from the rotting pears that had been touching the grass. I wrinkled my nose and frowned at Him. He twinkled at me, a little curve in one corner of His mouth.

"Yes?" He asked.

"Father, this tree has produced so much fruit, surely it is a good tree, so why is the fruit rotting?"

"This is a sturdy little tree, but it has presumed it can carry as much fruit as it can produce and it is not so. Fruit must be cared for or it will fall and rot."

Hmm, what is He getting at I wonder?

He took my arm again and we walked until we came to a mulberry. It was a pleasing shape with its winding trunk and branches full of large floppy leaves. There were berries upon berries; some a pale greenish white, some vibrant red and some like dark rich wine.

"This tree has produced fruit in keeping with its size and position. There is much that is ready and ripe, there is more that will ripen soon and there is yet more that will ripen later. I AM pleased with this tree."

Aha, I begin to see where this is going.

I smiled up at Him and caught Him eating a mulberry, the clear red juice dripping from His fingers.

"Come," He smiled, popping one into my mouth.

"There is more."

We stepped onto the grass and with the dew soaking into our shoes we stood before the wall that surrounded the fruit garden. Covering this side was an enormous fig; its large leaves hid the wall, the fruit and anything else that was growing beneath it. He began to lift some of the leaves and peer under them. I looked hard.

"I don't see anything but leaves Father."

He stepped back and gave me one of His patient looks.

"This years fruit is ripening nicely and next years is on the branch already. Just because you cannot see the fruit does not mean it is not there. Some fruits are more difficult to spot, you just have to know where to look."

I bent down and stepped underneath the branches, sparse rays of sunlight shone around me, picking out leaves and bulbous figs. They were well camouflaged, their colour matching perfectly with the leaves and branches. Next years fruit protruded in little green blobs and this years hung swollen and purpling.

"I see them" I exulted, pleased with myself.

"On we go then," He laughed.

And on we went.

In front of us was an apple tree, its branches were a perfect shape and not too heavily burdened that it was bending. Its leaves were small and numerous and its fruit was turning a delicious pink. A windfall squelched under my foot.

"This one looks good," I offered hopefully.

"Hmm."

He picked up a windfall and examined it thoughtfully.

I waited.

And yes here it comes.

"This tree has done well, but it has not held its fruit against the winds, nor protected them from parasites that sneak in and destroy."

Well you can't have everything!

His eyebrow raised slowly at me. I sat down on the wet grass with a flump.

"Sorry Father, but really, we try our best and it seems that nothing is good enough for You."

He laid His hand gently upon my head, His eyebrows returning to normal.

"You are right, nothing you can do is good enough, but you are wrong in that you presume that is what I look for."

I pondered this for a moment, then I asked, a little fearfully,

"What is it that You look for?"

"A heart willing to be loved."

❦ *PATTERNS* ❧

We ambled through the woodland, the rich smell of leaf mould all around us, I looked up through the canopy of red and gold at the rays of autumn light filtering over us.

Ooh, a little dizzy.

His strong hand closed around mine; the safety of His presence wrapping me in His warmth. I smiled up at Him gratefully.

"What are we doing today Father?"

"Patterns," He said cryptically.

Hmm, what does that mean?

I looked up, hoping for more but was disappointed. He was humming, purposely avoiding my eyes. I huffed.

How frustrating!

He huffed back mockingly and letting go of my hand, charged off into the trees laughing. He does play the best games! I gave chase, up hillock and down again I pursued Him, in and out of winding ways, through avenues of dripping branches. Finally I caught Him. Diving through a slightly prickly bush I grabbed the edge of His robe and hung on. Grass filled my mouth and tiny stones rattled against my teeth as He dragged me through the meadow.

"Stop, cheat!" I shouted, spitting out a bug.

Taking hold of my hand He lifted me like a feather and whisked me away with Him. We ran so fast that I could lift my feet off the ground and watch it whizz by beneath them. The wind pulled my hair away from my face and flapped my clothes against my body. It was clean, it was fresh and alive. Suddenly He stopped and I slammed into

Him. His arms enveloped me and I was lost in the folds of His garment. His hand touched my chin, tilting my face upwards. I gazed into Him and melted. After a long moment He turned me around. We were on the top of a steep hillock in the centre of the garden. From up here we had a panoramic view. Waves of treetops swayed below us. Pathways wound in spirals around clumps of barely covered bushes. Flower beds tiered downwards in a variety of shapes and sizes. There was a pleasing and patterned flow to the whole, which stretched as far as my eyes could see and beyond.

"Father it's absolutely enormous!"

"Oh it's not so big!" He chuckled. *"Maybe it is you that is small!"*

"Yes of course," an overwhelming and familiar feeling of insignificance crept up my throat.

"It is how I made you," He whispered gently.

I waited for more, I wasn't disappointed.

"Look closer."

My sight zoomed in like an opening telescope and I saw trees and bushes growing in fractals, self-replicating from their trunks to their branches to their veined leaves. A group of tall sunflowers with heads full of ripe seeds that flowed in unending opposing spirals. Near them, a full rose, its blousy bloom circling outwards in a perfect tier of soft peaches and cream. And closer I could see the veins in each petal, meandering into an estuary flowing into its centre. Even closer and I was looking at the formation of the molecules and their matching opposites. I gazed incredulous at the beauty of the miniscule created patterns that made up this one flower. My eyes retreated slowly and the vision grew wider until I was once more looking at the whole.

"Wow! I breathed out, "that was amazing!"

"Everything fits well, does it not?" He smiled.

My feelings of insignificance seemed insignificant.

✧ *RELOCATION* ✧

I stared numbly at the bare soil where the plant had been. Father had clearly said it did not fit in this part of the garden. The soil was not right, the light was not right and there was not enough drainage. So we moved it and now the bed looked deserted.

He had told me precisely where to meet Him today; the border by the potting shed. I waited, gazing numbly at the emptiness before me. Soft humming sounded behind me and there He was, waving the purple gardening gloves in my face.

Good, no mud up my fingernails today.

In His other hand was a tray filled with tiny green shoots poking their heads out of dark rich compost. Setting it down, we kneeled together at the edge of the bed. Poking a hole in the soil He re-planted a shoot, squished the mud around it and repeated the process, indicating I should copy. We worked with the babies, He planting in a line along the border in one direction and me in the other until the tray was empty and we were at opposite ends.

"All done Father," I called waving.

"Well come back then!" He yelled.

Well how was I supposed to know?

I blew a windy raspberry through my lips and stomped over to join Him.

"You quite finished relaxing?" He smiled, poking me in the ribs.

"Ouch!"

He's always laughing at me, am I so stupid?

A strong and safe arm slid around my shoulder, I sighed into Him, feeling silly.

"Sorry Father, I'm feeling a little sensitive for some reason."

He planted a kiss on the top of my head.

"Come on,"

He led me to the shed. Inside we found more trays with young plants, and more pots, some with fully grown bushes, others with pruned trees and still others with nothing growing.

"This is a very large shed, in fact Father it is much bigger that I thought."

I looked at all the tables covered in pots and trays reaching far into the distance.

"Yes, this is my relocation waiting shed, some of these should have been re-planted already but they were not willing."

"Eh?"

Things are just not falling into place today!

He held out His hands.

And now He wants the gloves back! I am really out of sorts!

He gazed at me thoughtfully, a little sadly maybe.

"Follow Me!"

He grabbed a large pot containing a prickly little bush.

Why am I getting the feeling this is somehow to do with me?

He marched, pot in one hand, me in the other. Feeling like a child I trotted to keep pace. Then He gave me that look again, the one where He knows something I don't. I stared uncomfortably as He took firm hold of the bush, tipped it from its pot and placed it carefully into a deep water filled hole in a nearby bed. My stomach churned with discomfort. He then scooped great handfuls of mud up around it and pressed down firmly. I felt sick!

"What's happening Father, what's wrong with me?"

I could feel myself starting to wretch.

"It is time to move on my child."

I don't want to hear this.

Wrenching my arms up, I covered my ears and shut my eyes tightly.

"And yet, if you want to follow Me, you must."

"Why?"

I was crying now, I loved my church, I loved the people, I knew them. They knew me. We had grown together for so long I could not bear to be without them. The years I had been with them played through my mind and I saw the wonderful times and the mediocre. I saw the love and the squabbles, the offerings we gave to Him and the ones we kept for ourselves and I knew a part of me would always be part of them wherever He put me. I came to a place of peace, a place of knowing that if He says so, all will be well. I looked Him square in the eyes.

"Yes," I said simply.

"Yes," He acknowledged smiling His sunshine all over me.

"Some of My children are planted in soil that does not have enough sustenance or the type of food required. Some have food to offer but it may not be needed or accepted. There are many stages of growth and each of them has needs and offerings. The place of planting therefore is

*consistently important and re-planting is not
something to be afraid of. When I AM the guide,
it is something to look forward to."*

❦ LOSS ❧

Wind howled in my ears. Hair lashed across my face. I tramped doggedly, my head down, through the storm that raged in the dark. Stinging rain sent wet rivers down my back.

Where am I? What's happening?

"Father, where are you?" I yelled, my voice snatched into nothing by the gale.

Pressing myself into a tree, the bark rough against my cheek, I clung on against the storm. Lightening streaked its shocking pathway through the darkness, lighting up a vision of cold fear.

Death was in the garden.

I watched him stalking, claiming, destroying. A scream ripped through the roaring thunder, my own throat defied control. Branches clawed at my arms and I ran, in blind panic with Death at my heels. My heart pounding in my chest, I gasped for breath as the thunder clashed and the lightening sheared the path before me. A soul wrenching crack and I fell, my knees sinking into sticky sod. A terrible groaning and crying filled the wind and I covered my ears. Skeletal shadows scratched at me as a tree crashed onto the path, shredded and scorched.

Instantly Death was there.

I froze in horror, my heart barely whispering its terrified prayer. "Help me."

"Fear not" His voice, so heavy with substance.

The air was split in two and the storm instantly silenced.

I watched in awe as Death slowly kneeled.

A strong Hand closed around mine and the light began to dawn, its clear bright rays soothing the battered garden. Breathing deeply, my heart thumping I saw Death take the tree with a touch and in obedience to the One who held me, release it into His hand. Fear and Death fled, leaving only the pain of loss behind.

That tree was where I had first met Him. It was the place I trusted I would always find Him, and now it was dead and gone. I broke. Sobs rose from a deep and locked up place, racking my body. He remained silently safe. When my storm had abated, anger took its place.

"How could You let that happen? You are supposed to love this garden! The loss is so great, I cannot bear it." I broke again and wept.

His fingers stroked my face softly and He looked deeply into my eyes. A great calm filled my heart and I was perfectly still.

"Yes, the loss is great, but the gain is far greater."

His hand gently turned my head and I saw a veil, like silken gossamer, descend from heaven. It parted a fraction, enough for me to catch a glimpse of within. And I saw the one I had lost and grieved for. She was standing beside her Saviour. They were arm in arm. She was glorious. Her face was bathed in golden light and her garments were like velvet rainbows that flowed and swirled around her. He stood in majestic joy, knowing this was the fulfilment of all her desires and His. I saw no shadow anywhere in that place, only everlasting and ever increasing life. A smile grew in my eyes, my cheeks crinkled with dried tears.

"Oh Father," was all I could utter, "Oh Father."

I must have fallen asleep in His arms, sitting up slowly I gazed at the dawn turning to dusk. The veil had melted away and the garden had returned to its earthly state. It seemed almost dull and grey in comparison. But then the shadow of death was in it. I felt His protection wrap around me like a thick blanket.

"For all My children, there is a time to be born and a time to die. All your days were written by Me before they came to be."

✄ LAID BARE ✄

I shivered and pulled my wrap tightly around my shoulders. Biting wind cut like a knife through every layer. Frozen mud pits crunched under my boots and a solitary robin sang a lonely but beautiful song as I clomped by. I breathed out fog like smoke before drying my lips on the back of my hand.

"At last!" He grinned at me and held out a hand.

"I came as soon as you called" I chattered through my teeth as I snugged up under His arm.

Ahh He's so warm.

I could feel Him chuckling, His body shaking gently as He drew me close.

"Today I want to show you something about loss."

I recoiled inside, why did I get the feeling this was going to be painful. Probably because it was!

We walked arm in arm, deeper into the garden. I marvelled at the spider's webs with iced teardrops hanging from every strand. Bushes and plants huddled together under blankets of frost. No animal stirred, apart from the robin who flew beside us. He darted in front, then waited in little hidden alcoves for us to catch up, before taking flight again and accompanying us deeper into the garden. We came to a stop in front of an ancient oak; its gnarled branches reached towards the light shamelessly naked. Not a leaf remained on any part. Its structure was entirely exposed. I felt a little awkward, intrusive almost. I stood blinking stupidly, huffing into my hands as a distraction. I was stalling, He knew it and I knew it.

"This is a beautiful tree, is it not?" One of His eyebrows rose in a question I was not required to answer.

I waited, allowing His comment to redirect my thoughts.

"When all is stripped away, the core is revealed."

I risked a glance. His Face was thoughtful, serious but not sad. I waited again, preparing myself for what was coming.

"And the true nature is revealed."

We stood facing the oak. He moved behind me and wrapped His arms around me. Warmth flooded my cold body. I breathed with memories of loss; of times when all my comforts and supports had been taken from me, when I had been stripped bare of all I had leaned on, and my gnarled character had been left exposed. Leaving only Him to reach for. Only Him who loved.

I gazed at the tree in a new way. All of its beauty invisibly held within. A life force that delved deeper in the winter, pulsing within the core of the tree and pushing down into the roots to strengthen the inner life. The robin perched on a low branch and suddenly burst into song. Light filled my heart and memories settled into thankfulness. He squeezed me tighter.

"I will never leave you."

❧ *SEASONS* ❧

We were sitting reminiscing and reflecting on the past year of lessons in the garden. He squeezed my hand and spoke a single Word.

"Spring."

Images of fresh yellows and greens danced across my vision. The joy of new shoots bursting out of dew soaked earth. Light breezes carrying the scent of sun drenched showers. The sound of the birds singing their songs of love and courtship.

Spring brings hope, it is filled with the eagerness of life and the energy of new growth. Everything about it is fresh and bursting, it is truly filled with joy and spurts of exulting praise.

A contented sigh puffed its way out of my cheeks. He chuckled beside me, a deep throaty chuckle.

How He loves me.

"Summer."

His strong voice interrupted my wanderings and my mind cascaded with heady scents of rose and honeysuckle. Blues and lilacs, rich reds and delicate pinks, full blooms dripping with warm rains. The flurry of creation pro-creating and caring for its offspring, from the tiny fruit filling with liquid sunlight to the wild ones that rollick and romp with fluffy faces.

I love the summer, it is full of heat and nurture, of ripening fruits and maturing growth. It brings wholeness, creation completes itself in the summer.

My face relaxed into an easy smile as I lay back on the grass gazing at the wisps of angel shaped clouds swimming across the blue.

"Autumn."

He spoke again and my vision changed.

I saw trees dressed as royalty in all the colours of fire. Reds and golds, flickering oranges and frost kissed yellows. Reaching their arms wide they cast their fluttering treasures to the wind. Their fragrance of abandonment nourishing the ground for those who came after. An abundance of jewelled berries and nuts, provided rich pickings for the small creatures that tend the garden. Ripe plump fruits, leaked juice, for all to revel in and enjoy. A thousand seeds catapulted into the sky, freed from their earthly bonds to find good soil and become next season's creatures.

Autumn is the time of settled maturity, the time when the promise of fruit is fulfilled and all is infused with a tranquil beauty. Yet there is something solemn about the autumn; it makes me sad but I don't know why. Maybe it's the dying leaves or perhaps it's because it means saying goodbye to so much in the garden.

I wriggled uncomfortably.

"Winter."

I shivered at His Word.

That's why autumn makes me sad, it's because I know winter is coming.

Winter. When all the animals hide from the biting cold that strips the garden bare. Anything left is frozen until all its life is buried deeply in the earth and only skeletal echoes remain. For a short time snow is winters beauty. Its white blanket brings a purity unseen at any other time of the year. And it waters the ground with life.

I know the winter is necessary, the garden needs to rest, it needs a time where it grows deeper and the surface growth dies back. But I know that these winters weigh heavy in my heart. I have seen many and there will be more.

"And then it will be spring again."

His voice was almost a whisper, His words hung between us like beacons of hope. The song of an approaching blackbird lifted the heaviness.

"Yes Father, You always make it spring again."

His hand rested gently on my head. Comfort covered me like softly falling feathers.

"You think I AM too hard on my children?"

There was no point answering, He knew what I was thinking.

"I know how strong you are, better even than you know it yourselves. I know the beauty that lies within each of you and I AM determined for you to be all that I created you to be. Every season has My purpose intricately woven into it. Nothing is left to chance and nothing is wasted. In My Garden there is a time and a way to perfect everything and I will do it in spite of your struggles."

My heart pounded in my chest with the revelation of the uncompromising strength of His Love.

✂ *FALSEHOOD* ✄

We had stepped momentarily outside the gate.
As I looked around at this different garden, a
strange feeling of familiarity crept over me.

"Father, this looks like…"

"Does it? Does it really?"

"Well, yes and no."

What seemed to be a copy of the inner garden
was somehow out of sync. The flowers were large
and garish, full of loud but shallow colour and
without scent. The closer I looked the more ugly
they were. Bushes fought with each other for sun

space, strangling anything in their way. Sharp and jagged stones rose with forced effort from the rockery, aggressively slicing through the plant growth. A slither of unease crawled up my neck, the hairs prickling with it. He squeezed my hand and held it firmly, reassuringly.

This is a strange and dangerous place, it looks like His Garden, but it is not.

As far as my eyes could see, this garden appeared to be full of growth and flamboyant colour, but on closer inspection the plants were sick. Some of them rotting from the inside, others suffocating smaller growth as they used them to climb higher. Nausea rose in my throat and my brain rattled about inside my head.

"What is this place?"

I stared at Him, my face wearing revulsion like a mask.

"This is a falsehood. Those that are planted here have been seduced by something that looks like the truth but is not the truth."

"Why? How did this happen?"

"They desired Me to do their will and when I did not, they were seduced by that which promised it would."

The feeling of nausea reached my mouth and I retched involuntarily. His hand held me fast.

"What can be done Father, please do something to save them," The retch became a sob and tears dripped from my chin.

"They must remember how it was at first and face the truth of their deception. Only when they stop rushing from here to there pursuing what they imagine to be the pleasure of My Presence will they realise..."

"It is not always a pleasure!" I finished the sentence before I could stop myself. "Well it's true, sometimes Your Presence is painful."

He smiled, a soft gentle sad smile.

I grimaced at the instant insistence of my reaction.

Why do I do that?

"I'm sorry Father," I squeezed His Hand, pained that I had hurt Him with the blunt truth of the gospel according to me!

"Only then will they realise….. I AM within."

∽ SUN GAZERS ∾

As I sat in the middle of the grass my eyes
scanned the radiant colours all around me. Dust
particles glittered across my vision through shafts
of filtered sunlight and the buzzing of insects
lulled me into a semi-sleep state. I vaguely
noticed shadowy sections where the flowers bent
their heads to the ground, and next to them,
bright pools of light where the faces of the
flowers shone back at the sun. Sinking into the
soft grass, the blades tickling my bare arms, I let
my eyelids fall. Undiluted rays seeped into my
skin warming me to my bones.

This is the life.

A breath of fragrant air and He was beside me, laying in the grass. His radiance even brighter than the sun. Heat and glory enveloped me and I glowed with the reflection of Him.

"Oh Father, this is where I would be forever, beside You."

"Oh really?" His mouth twitched at the corner.

Well that woke me up.

"What do you mean?" I asked slightly offended.

"Look around you, tell me what you see."

Uh oh, here we go!

"I see glorious flowers bathing in sunlight. I see other flowers in shadow, hmm, and they are not so glorious….,"

My voice deserted me. I had missed the point; it was the eyebrow that gave it away.

"We will wait awhile."

And that was all the explanation I got!

The sun moved slowly across the sky, weaving in and out of ripples of clouds. His hand went to mine and we lay there, almost content for hours.

An inquisitive butterfly fluttered in my face, startling me out of a dreamy doze.

"What?" I mumbled. He patted my hand.

"What do you see now?"

The sun was almost down; its last few drops rested on the shadowed flowers.

Wow!

What a transformation. They were beauties. Perfectly formed heads swayed in rhythm together, lifting and falling with the slight breeze. Layers of aqua and blue within each petal gave them a depth like the sky reflected in the sea. And the scent; the soft breath carried it towards us, like dew drenched honey.

"They are beautiful Father."

"Yes, they are, and what about the others?"

He nodded in the direction of the sun gazers.

"Where are they?" I blurted, surprise in my open mouth.

"Shrivelled beyond recognition."

"Why? What happened?" This one really had me going. I had no idea what He was getting at.

"The beauties have cultivated their inner life and know how to survive the shadows. The sun gazers chased the external glory and as a consequence have no depth."

✺ *PRUNING* ✺

I stumbled along, teeth chattering against the wind that cut like an icy knife through my clothes and burned my skin with its frozen fingers.

"Brrrr, Father where are You?"

Unbelievable! Yesterday was so beautiful and He had been so present. Where is He? I don't want to play hide and seek.

The dark sky weighed heavy on me, filled as it was with approaching storms. I huddled miserably under the bough of a large oak.

"Father, where are You?" I shouted but the wind whipped my voice into a whisper.

Leaning in I soldiered on battling from one tree to the next. In and out of bushes that grasped at me. Slippery wet leaves moved treacherously beneath my feet. Clumps of coarse grass tripped me, my ankles twisting in pitted and sunken pot holes. I fell more than once. My wrap was lost, my hair matted tangles, my clothes stiff with wet clay. Desperately I searched. He was not there. He was nowhere! My heart caved into the empty void. All that was in me cried out. A gut wrenching wail worked its way up from my depths and out through my mouth. My legs buckled and soft mud squelched around the knees of my corduroys as I hit the ground. Burying my face in my hands I whimpered, broken. Hours passed. I lay there sodden and freezing, uncaring about all but the loss of His Presence.

All I want is Him. All I ever wanted was Him. Without Him there is nothing. Without Him I can't go on.

I drifted into a world of dreams where I was alone, pursued by terrifying creatures seeking my destruction.

"Father!" I cried out in my semi-conscious state.

I sank deeper into the dream. Darkness was there. Thick darkness. A Presence in its centre. His Presence, waiting, silently knowing all. A great stillness filled my soul and I knew He had always been there with me. Light slowly dawned and I understood. He was not the euphoria. He was not the pain. He was not the light nor the water. He was in it all but it was not Him. He was more than all of them. He was all there really was.

I awoke in a warm sunlit grove surrounded by gently swaying willows. The sound of bubbling streams weaved around the trees and a song-thrush sang its gentle flute like song nearby. The scent of fresh clean grass filled the air.

"How are you feeling?"

My heart sang with the bird, He was there, beside me.

"A little tender," I looked longingly at Him and He drew me closer.

We sat together in silence for some time, my heart healing. I had so many questions but could not verbalise even one.

"When you are young, I nurture your growth like a tiny shoot, tenderly encouraging and gently feeding you,"

He was going to answer my unspoken questions.

A contented sigh deflated my chest.

"As you grow, I prune you of all that is not of Me. I cut away your dead and diseased growth, freeing and purifying you."

My delight in the external feelings of His Presence flitted through my mind. Startled, I realised they were not Him; they were me. I had been hungering for more of them, not more of Him.

"Ooh," I gasped uncontrollably. His arm tightened.

"As many times as is necessary."

I felt an ache in my soul; a sweetness permeated from it, seeping painfully into my body.

"Your pain is your healing after your pruning."

"Thank you," I whispered. Grateful in the knowledge that He will save me, even from myself.

∽ *SEEDS* ⁊

"Meet Me at the poly tunnel."

I awoke with His words in my ears.

I roused myself and prepared to search out the poly tunnel. It wasn't difficult to find; the reflection of the sun on the white plastic dome gave it away at some distance. Although, if I hadn't been looking for it, I wouldn't have ventured into this part of the garden. All around me were small regular shaped beds each housing plant groups of different types and at different stages of growth. There were tools leaning against fences, upturned wheelbarrows and pots stacked here and there. It wasn't the tidiest or the prettiest part of the garden. It was a working environment, dangerously so in some places. I skirted a particularly sharp looking pickaxe on the path. He was leaning against the open door of the poly tunnel, arms folded and smiling at me dodging His tools. My cheeks lifted in response.

"Come and see," He said turning and entering the tunnel. The plastic crackled as the opening fell closed behind us.

The tunnel was long and narrow with a warm earthy smell. A brick path cut through the middle of rows of waist height tables. On top of the tables were trays, plant pots of all shapes and sizes, glass jars, packets and buckets. Underneath the tables were bags of soil of various colours, watering cans and some were boxed in to make cupboards. I took it all in while I waited for Him to enlighten me.

"What do you see?"

It's going to be one of those days!

"I don't see any gloves!" I retorted, feeling clever. He ignored me and waited. Feeling clever never lasts long with Him around.

"I see pots, soil, watering cans, and trays," an idea struck me, like a mallet. "What do you see Lord?" Now I felt really clever. Ha gotcha!

"Look closer," He said firmly and with a hint of 'stop messing about' in His tone.

I moved nearer to one of the tables. Along the back was a row of little pots with clear lids; in them were different seeds. Aha!

"Seeds Father, I see seeds."

"Finally," He breathed, looking at me with His eyes wide.

I felt stupid! And then He wrapped His arms around me and squeezed until I felt loved and slightly breathless.

"Tell me about them, please."

We walked, arm in arm through the centre of the tunnel.

"I love this place of beginnings, it is a joy to Me."

I looked at the passing table, on it were trays of tiny shoots.

"These have been waiting for germination through two seasons of winter and now they are ready. See how strong their tiny stems are. They are determined in their growth."

I remembered several winters in my own life and the determination they brought about within me.

The next table had several strategically placed mirrors on it and a cupboard encasing the legs. We stopped and He adjusted one of the mirrors; behind it I noticed a soil filled seed tray.

"These are those that need the light to bring about their birth."

A friend came to mind. How her face had shone when she had first met Him! How His light had been the birthing instrument in her life. The beauty of the memory made me smile. He jolted me back with a sharp knock on the cupboard doors.

"In here are seeds that will only grow when they are plunged into the deepest darkness."

His words resonated in my heart; dark times I would not want to repeat but neither did I want to give up the grace that had grown in me as a result. I was stronger and my faith was firmer because of them. I realised with a surprising joy that I was thankful for them. He touched my arm gently and pointed.

"Some seeds must be dried as part of the germination process."

Thousands of tiny seeds had been spread out on sheets laid in trays, drying and warming. I could see them breaking away from their parent plant, almost to the point of death by drought. And then, at His perfect time, they were ready to spring into life. I thought of my own children and my heart caught in my throat.

"And on this table are seeds that must be immersed before planting."

There were buckets full of water which on closer inspection contained large floating seeds.

Yes, I understand, there are times we all need immersing before a growth spurt.

He suddenly turned from the path into another plastic side door which led to a mini poly tunnel. A wall of intense heat smothered me. My lungs burned as I breathed in and sweat prickled from every pore.

"Phew, it's hot in here," I clung on to His robe.

"Yes, the seeds in here need heat to release the life hidden within, whereas the seeds in here," we passed through another door, *"need cold."*

The blast of freezing air was momentarily a relief from the heat but almost instantly my sweat turned to ice and I shivered uncontrollably. I clutched at Him desperately. He led me out and back into the original tunnel.

"That wasn't the most pleasant experience Father."

"Indeed," He answered, with a look that said, 'and why do you think that is?'

I don't know, what has heat and cold to do with seeds and growth? Aha!

The light dawned! Extreme and sometimes unpleasant circumstances are just tools for growth.

"Seeds are interesting, are they not?"

Here it comes.

"There are so many varieties and each of them needs their own particular environment to germinate and grow. All my children are individual and I know exactly what to do and when to do it. In My Hands, everything is made beautiful."

Don't you just love Him!

ɕ *THE MAZE* ɞ

Slowly my senses became aware. My chest
swelled with breath. Heat spread over my back.
Dark wood focussed before my eyes. A large
oaken door stood before me edged by vast
evergreens that stretched as far as I could see on
either side.

"Father?" I queried.

Instantly I was aware of Him behind me, towering
over me, protecting me on all sides. Turning, I
buried my face in Him. His arms circled me and I
was encased in love.

"Within this maze are many paths. Your direction is your decision, but remember, there are consequences to every choice."

He turned me to face the door. It swung silently inward. I stepped through the opening and the door shut behind me. I was alone outwardly, but inwardly I knew Him. Or so I thought!

Before me were three pathways leading into the hedged maze. I studied each of them carefully. To my right was a wide green path, its hedges bright with sunlight. Many colours bloomed further down, intertwined with the evergreens. Its invitation to 'Come in' was warm and delicious. The path directly in front of me was more of a tunnel, dark with twisting vines covering the roof and leaves so thick that they repelled the light. I could only see a little way and it seemed to grow with darkness. In fact it shouted, 'Stay out!' The third of the pathways lay to my left. It was not as wide as the sunlight path but it was clear; the sun casting rays between the hedgerows. Its floor was covered with newly laid pale woodchip and forget-me-not's sprinkled blue along the edges. 'I'm safe,' it whispered and I made my decision.

My feet crunched softly on the woodchip. All around me was green. At my feet the small blue flowers grew amongst the scattered bark. I plodded steadily along, waiting for some enlightened God moment. Everything was beautiful and natural. I could hear distant birds chirping. A couple of rabbits bobbed about further down the path, their white tails flashing as I caught up with them and they darted through the hedge. All around me was good and I walked contentedly for several hours. I passed other paths that veered off like branches to the left and right. Some were overlaid with dark and leafy canopies. Some very bright with flowers blooming in the high hedges. One was even a precarious looking rope bridge. I snorted. I wasn't going to be led off the path by that! After some time the light began to dim.

How much further is it?

Darkness crept up the hedges on both sides and the path narrowed.

"Ouch," a twig snatched at my face.

My fingers touched stickiness.

I must be bleeding.

It was growing so dark that I could barely see. My hands reached for either side to reassure me of my direction. Thorns scratched across my palms without mercy, drawing more blood. Nervousness rose in my throat and I moved faster. Branches tore at me, twisting themselves in my hair and wrenching it out.

"Oow!" I shouted angrily slapping at the sides. Suddenly my face was crushed into hedge and tiny leaves filled my open mouth. It was a dead end!

Oh no, this was the wrong path!

I sat down and spat out the inedible greenery in desperate frustration.

I'll have to go back.

Growling, I scrambled up. Branches pressed in on me and as I shuffled away from them I found them pressing me on the other side. With shock I watched as the dark hedges closed in, cutting me off from any way back and imprisoning me in a tangled mass of twining branch and leaf. Needles reached out, scratching and piercing me in a thousand places. I curled into a ball and cried out exasperated.

"Father, help me, where are You?"

Silence.

The realisation that the path had been a distraction slowly dawned. Now that it was no longer pleasing, I could see it was the wrong path. I was stuck, pressed on all sides, no hope of going backwards, forwards or any other way!

What an idiot, stupid, proud, idiot!

An empty void gnawed at my insides, I was alone, outwardly and inwardly. Humbled and bleeding I entreated Him.

"Father, I'm on the wrong path, please help me."

I felt the bush part and a Hand reached down to lift me. I only saw the Hand but I remember it was covered in scratches. Once I was on my feet again, He was gone. I was faced with two more paths: one, a familiarly dark tunnel, the other a stairway cut into the hedge, its steps leading up and above the maze. The stairway invited me with its promise of clear sight.

I will not be so easily lured by my own judgement this time. I am not to be trusted with choices. I am too self-centred and move unconsciously to that which appeals to my senses.

"Father, how do I know which is the best path for me? The right path for me? Your path for me?"

I distinctly heard an approving grunt. I warmed inside and the void was filled with Him once more.

"Take a single step and listen within."

I obeyed, choosing the stairway. With the first step I heard birds and a gentle breeze rustling the leaves. I shut out the external and listened within. The fullness was diminished and a slight unrest was creeping in. I stepped down instantly. Crouching I half hopped, half bounced into the dark leafy tunnel and listened. Externally was thick with silence, dense and impenetrable. Internally, however, my fullness overflowed and I glowed with a sense of peace and rightness.

How amazing, I have an internal compass.

I scooted up the tunnel to the sound of Him chuckling. It was long and it was dark but I hardly noticed because of the fullness in my heart. As morning approached I came out into a wide place of lush green grass with a round brick well in its centre. There He was, sitting on the wall holding a ladle filled with the water of life and waiting for me. Whilst I drank deeply, I noticed the scars on both of our hands.

❧ *CAGES* ❧

"Mmm, raspberries are gorgeous," I wiped at the juice trickling down my chin and groped for another.

I was sitting under the raspberry canes near the poly-tunnel. Father was nowhere to be seen so I thought I'd try a few early ripening berries while I waited for Him.

"Hey there young lady, are you going to gorge yourself on those all day or would you like to follow Me?"

I ask you, what kind of a question is that! I poked my head up through the raspberries and came face to face with Him.

"Oh, hello," I grinned, my mouth stained a rich raspberry red. He chortled back. I joined Him on His walk, we waltzed, our arms swinging in time.

We arrived at an avenue of ornamental cherries, their pink petticoats long gone. Sauntering between them we came to several large metal framed cages, each one the size of a small swimming pool. He opened the door to one and ushered me through. I stood in the center and turned slowly, studying the inside of the cage. Sunlight fell in stripes through wooden slats which ran around the bottom four feet; covering that and rising up the sides and over the roof was rather deadly looking wire mesh.

I wouldn't want to be a bird caught up in that.

"No indeed!"

I'm not sure I like having my every thought listened in on. Frowning, I took a deep breath and plunged.

"So Father, why are we here?"

"That is a very large question and not one I'm going to answer today." He grinned at me, with a hint of playfulness.

I tutted, loudly. I'm not in the mood for games today. His large hand stroked my hair, covering the top of my head completely. I feel small and I've got stomach ache, probably from too many raspberries. His hands grabbed my waist and the warm wind rushed into my face as He lifted me and swung me around, my arms and legs flapping against each other in a very undignified display. He put me down gently and a single tear squeezed itself out of the corner of my eye.

What is the matter with me today?

"What do you see?"

Oh please don't let it be a cryptic afternoon.

"What do you see?" He repeated a little more loudly and a good deal more firmly.

"Umm, a cage with a tree in it."

Why is it in a cage?

"And why do you think I have planted it in a place where it is restricted?"

"I don't know," I muttered.

"Look closely at it, what else do you see?"

"It's a cherry tree, I see cherries, lots of cherries."

"Yes, lots of fruit," He opened the cage and led me outside.

"Now what do you see?"

There were places where the tree had poked a branch out through the mesh.

"There are branches growing through the wire, towards the light?" I felt myself grow a little taller. His eyes bored into my soul like fire. I knew I was missing the point, I was definitely tuned out today.

"Yes, the tree would prefer to grow wildly unrestricted. What else do you see?"

"Nothing!"

"What, no fruit?" He was right, there was no fruit on the branches outside the cage, not even one cherry.

"Why is there no fruit?" I asked incredulous and completely in the dark.

"The cage is restricting, but it is also protecting. The cage prevents the fruit from being consumed by those it is not intended for."

My stomach settled and my mind raced into action. So many times in my life I had felt thwarted. Now I wondered, how many of those were times He'd saved me from my wild self?

Something else flickered across my consciousness. The times when I had been hurt by my own wild choices and He had not restricted me.

"Why don't You protect me all the time?"

"My daughter, though it hurts us both, sometimes it is the only way."

"Then why do you save me at all?" I was feeling decidedly sassy now.

"I will not and cannot allow more than you can bear."

I may not be tuned in but He is never tuned out. He gets me every time.

~THE GARDEN'S HEART~

My heart awoke to whisperings not my own.

"Come, I want to show you the life and soul of the garden."

I rose in a dream. I knew this part of the garden existed but I had seen it only from afar. It lay central and surrounded by high hedges that obscured its secret. Wearing only my nightgown, I padded softly behind Him with bare feet. A blood moon cast an orange glow, lighting up the blades of grass like fire. Expectancy hung thickly in the air around us like an impending storm. His robes swished silently in front. Breathing shallow gasps,

I followed closer. The high hedge towered before us dark and forbidding. He held open a door and, standing aside, guided me through. Alone and hemmed in. I knew this was His plan, that I should follow this path of shadows to His very heart. Each step was a lifetime of journeying. Moving slowly, I recounted my life like a vision playing itself before my eyes. Father was far from me. I shrank from His memory, shrivelling inside. With each turn of the path a jolt of historic shame added its weight to my back until I was crawling on all fours, cloying mud hardening beneath my nails and in the creases of my palms. I crawled blind. My face in the dirt. My humour died the death of exposure and a new fear grew within me.

Will I make it?

Quaking, I reached the centre and lay prostrate in the mud. A hand reached down and lifted me to His face. I was undone, laid bare, in all my shame. He saw my all. Before I could cover my face He grasped my hands and turned me firmly to the core. A wooden stake grew straight up, reaching higher than I could see, the soil melted at its foot and I gaped into transparent earth at roots that went deeper than my sight. From the base there flowed a river of blood. I struggled against His strength. He stepped into the flow dragging me with Him, wide eyed and trembling. I had no courage of my own. I would have fallen if He were not holding me. The blood swirled around my feet, soaking through my skin and into the bone. And He was ever silent in His strength and determination. As I drowned in blood He began to glow. His radiance was so bright I could see Him through closed eyelids, shining in all His terrifying glory.

The blood became the water and the journeys of my life were washed into purity. My shame was undone and He was laid bare. I succumbed to a world of whirling colour which saturated me to my core, unmaking and recolouring my story. We walked out the way I had come; the same but different. Hand in hand. The evergreens extended their playful scent to sooth and perfume us. Father was waiting beyond the door to embrace us. The Son and the daughter.

❧ REFLECTIONS ❧

'Good morning,' His voice whispered softly in my inner ear.

I yawned, my arms and mouth stretching wide in unison.

With a somewhat foggy demeanour I mumbled, "Good morning Father, what shall I wear today, are we digging or mudslinging?"

"Walking."

I donned jeans, jumper and my walking boots.

How far? I wondered, entering the garden.

He smiled, a warm welcoming smile, and took my hand.

"No gloves?" He teased. I giggled, elated with the ease of our interaction.

Today feels like a simple day, without too many deep contemplations or complications.

Famous last thoughts!

We walked hand in hand, our arms swinging towards a clear path that cut its way through the garden like the edge of a knife; straight and clean. My legs wobbled as we stepped onto it, and He held me upright. The path was moving like a conveyor belt, slowly through the trees. Bushes coasted by. Different scents drifted past, creating a concoction of perfumes I was unable to distinguish into single smells.

"Let's walk," He announced and as we moved the garden gathered speed, sailing by in a flurry of greens and browns all mixing into a blur.

"Whoa!!" My dizzy brain blurted.

"Let's run!" He yelled, squeezing my hand tightly as He pulled me along behind Him. We raced

through the garden. Lines of landscape flew by, too fast for my eyes to register their form or speed. Suddenly we catapulted out into the world beyond. He stopped abruptly and I crashed into the back of Him.

"Oouf!"

"Look around you," He commanded.

I obeyed, too flustered to argue. The path slowed to conveyor belt speed once more and I was able to watch the world around us pass like a film. A man laying himself as a bridge for others to cross to safety. A boy pinning a girl against a wall and violating her. A woman weeping over her lost children. A father seeking revenge. A teacher protecting children from bullets by taking them into her own body. Men, women, children, in their frailty and their strength, jostling together for space. Holding each other. Hating each other. Loving each other. It was heaven and it was hell. My heart thumped against my ribs and I looked at Him. There were tears in His eyes and burying my face in His robe, I wept for His pain.

"I don't want to see any more," My voice sounded small and distant.

"If you want to help, you must see."

He gently but firmly turned me outwards and held me against Him, His arms wrapped across my chest. Feeling safely swaddled I slowly opened my eyes. The moving path continued and I saw what He saw. We are created amazing! We have the life and breath of God in us! It is not so much what we suffer but how we suffer! I saw how some of the world reflected the garden and I saw how some of the garden reflected the world. I looked at Him shocked.

"Now you see, this too is My garden."

✥ *BEING* ✥

As I opened the door, rays of sunlight crashed over me like white horsed waves on the beach. I stepped onto the soft green carpet and a host of chattering sparrows lifted from a nearby bush and fluttered away.

I wonder where He is.

My thoughts trailed deliciously around Him. His voice with its quiet but total authority. His touch and how it always calms me. His playful humour. His delight with me even when I am unlovely.

How amazing He is. Hmm, amazing and absent.

It was true, He was definitely absent and I had wandered without thinking to the place we last sat together. A small and sheltered hillock hiding a copse of young trees with fragrant blossoms, their scent drifting around me in the warm breeze. A large bumble bee hummed impossibly into view. I watched it bob about and disappear into a fox glove trumpet, its muffled hum fading in and out. Scanning the area with my senses, I could see, and feel, He wasn't here.

"Where are you Father?"

A heavy silence filled my ears. Tutting I continued my search, walking a little quicker to another part of the garden, the part we had planted seeds.

"Father?"

The silence grew louder.

How strange. He is always here somewhere. Why can't I find him? Have I done something wrong?

I searched my heart as I walked to yet another of the places we had met and worked. But there was nothing I could think I may have done that would have offended Him. The sudden clapping of dove's wings in startled flight made me jump as I entered the ring of rose bushes, the last place I could think He might be. He was not there.

I don't understand, Father? I sat in the centre of the ring and stroked the hair like grass with my palms.

I cannot find Him so I will wait and perhaps He will find me.

Slowly my heart and my mind stilled. I was aware of the distant scurrying of small creatures through undergrowth, the tickling of the grass on my legs, the coolness of the ground beneath me and the heady smell of the roses as they enticed their treasure bearers. And then, a deep echo moved within me.

"Be still and I will draw you to Myself."

Relief flooded me. I lay back smiling and stared at the sapphire sky.

"At last, I knew you were here somewhere."

"Allow yourself to slow and be still. Trust and wait on Me. I will draw you to My Presence within yourself."

I shifted, stretched out my arms, untangled my legs and waited in stillness. The silence surrounding me made my skin tingle as it penetrated, seeping into every crevice of awareness and soaking into the depths of my heart and soul. And then I felt the slow and definite call of His Presence, drawing me inward, turning my vision central and growing in strength with my focus. Almost instantly I was there, in the place of fullness of Him. In the very core of my being He was waiting. And there we dwelt, together. There was no doing, only being.

❦ THE FLOWER ❧

"You have cut your hair," somehow the statement made me wriggle inside.

I looked up at Him. I was right, He was looking at me with a slightly pained expression. I waited for more.

"Why?"

I cringed and thought about my friend and her opinion that my long hair was making me look older.

"It makes me look younger!"

It's my hair!

My defence hackles rose. He smiled and my defences crumbled.

"Come with Me, I want to show you something."

I slipped my hand in His and walked beside Him, my heart pounding and my breath short.

This is going to hurt, I just know it.

We ducked through an avenue of low hanging branches covered with deep pink sprays of fragrant blossom swinging in the soft breeze. With every step my eyes widened and my skin tingled.

Wow! What is this place?

We came out into a living cave covered in the same rose coloured flowers. I gazed up at Him, my chest heaving with the raw life filling the chamber.

"It is the power of creation you are feeling. This is the womb of the garden where all is created. You are going to create a flower for My garden."

"I am?" the words fell out of my open mouth.

"You are."

We knelt facing each other and He took both my hands in His. A warm glow began in the centre of my being and I saw in my mind's eye the sprouting of a shoot. As I watched, it grew and became a stalk with leaves that protruded at intervals. He squeezed my hands.

"Now it is your turn."

I focused on the stalk, on the life coursing up its centre. A bud began to form at its top. Slowly I imagined its opening and colour, the great flopping purple veined shape of the petals and the overwhelming fullness of their heavy scent that could fill any garden. I was enjoying myself.

I will make a flower that is more beautiful than any of the others!

A yellow centre with pollen like gold dust emerged and at the edge of every flouncing petal a flame like fire. So large was the head of the flower that it engulfed its stalk, reaching almost to the ground.

"Come forth!" He commanded.

I saw the flower become a reality before my eyes. I held it in my hands and with a hint of reluctance offered it to Him. He was wearing gloves! He took it from me and holding it high, I saw it standing within the garden, dwarfing the other plants with its garish colour and its cloying scent.

"It is ugly!" I announced.

"It is vanity!" He pronounced.

"I don't understand, it looked better when I was making it."

"Watch!" He commanded holding up the flower again and as I stared the gaudy petals fell away, revealing the original shoot. It slowly unfolded to reveal a single flower with delicate petals that fell in long pale pink waterfalls from a golden heart.

"Beautiful," I breathed.

"And the scent?" He waved it under my nose, releasing a freshness that sang of clear springs and morning dew.

"More beautiful," I exclaimed, lost in wonder.

He held it high and I saw it once more take its place in the garden. This time it subtleties blended perfectly with its surroundings neither dominating nor dwarfing but complementing and adding something that was not there before. We sat in silence for some time. I got the distinct feeling He was waiting for me to catch up somehow. I looked up at His face quizzically.

"My way is always best."

The comparison of the two flowers spun around my head.

Of course, next to His work who do I think I am that I can make anything that comes close?

I had made what I thought would be an improvement on His creation. A feeling of self-disgust crept over me.

"Father I am so sorry."

"Why?" He touched the ends of my shortened hair and the question hung before me, inviting me to search myself for the answer.

Why had I cut my hair? When did this vanity start? I remembered as a child being called 'pretty', and as the years went by the wordy judgments of others became 'attractive' and 'beautiful hair'. I thought of those who were not considered 'attractive' and those who were. The judgments of others resulted in the same vanity. I had self-created in the image of others judgments. The light began to dawn and I noticed He was smiling. Warm and unconditional love radiated from Him, encouraging me further in my soul-searching. Those years of gaudy clothing and make-up, the cover of exotic perfumes, even the character development was to serve the opinions of others in order to make myself pleasing to them.

"Why?" I repeated.

He touched my heart with the tips of His fingers, He was gloveless again. I searched deeper. I wanted to belong. It was as simple as that.

"You belong to Me," His words poured through His fingertips. The power of new creation like liquid gold filled my heart, freeing me from the enslavement of vanity. How wonderfully He saves!

⚞ ONENESS ⚟

A fresh breeze ruffled my hair and the scent of young green shoots playfully tickled my nostrils. A hand beckoned me through an avenue of fluttering willows, their leaves brushed coolly across my face. I followed into a meadow of grass swaying lushly amongst flowers. Scattered heads of cornflower blue, pockets of sun kissed daisies, rich reds and golden yellows danced together in the breeze. I walked, softly stroking their upturned faces, my palms tingling at their touch. The scent of summer flowed around me in a warm haze. A tiny pop and a flower set itself free from its binding stem to swirl up towards the light. And then a thousand pops and the air erupted with blooms bursting from their earthbound homes, cascading upwards in a fountain of colour and fragrance. Laughing I swirled and skipped, singing and dancing with the living day stars that whirled their beauty all about me.

In the centre of the meadow, in the brightest undiluted sunlight, I found Him.

The long grass around Him had been flattened by giggling children rolling and playing together. I sat with Him and the children moved on, their unrestrained joy fading. Suddenly His strong hands were around me, propelling me over and over in the grass and then He was next to me, His face above mine. His eyes held me so deeply I lay helpless and unable to move. His kiss wrenched my heart to the surface and I was utterly consumed.

✎ *AWAKENING* ✎

The following morning I stood and looked out of the window at the world, His wider garden and my 'commission'. The world stared back, pleading with me to put on my gardening gloves and get stuck in. And there on the window ledge, as plain as day, lay a pair of purple gardening gloves.....

✎ *THE BEGINNING* ✎

TITLES IN THIS SERIES

⅋ *THE GARDEN* ⁊

⅋ *THE GARDEN BEYOND* ⁊

⅋ *THE GARDEN WITHIN* ⁊

Copies available from
www.christart.co.uk/books.html
www.amazon.co.uk